Ready… set… go green!

CREDITS

Words and Pictures: Kevin Airgid
Editor: Crona Airgid
Leo Puppet: Thistledown Puppets
Leo Photography: Steve Pomerleau

This book and its content are protected by international copyright law. This book and its content may not be copied, published, distributed, downloaded or otherwise stored in a retrieval system, transmitted or converted, in any form or by any means, electronic or otherwise, without the prior written permission of the copyright owner.

© 2009, Airgid Media Inc.

For — Onya, Ronan, and Keira

"Grown-ups never understand anything for themselves, and it is tiresome for children to be always and forever explaining things to them."
— Antoine de Saint-Exupery, The Little Prince

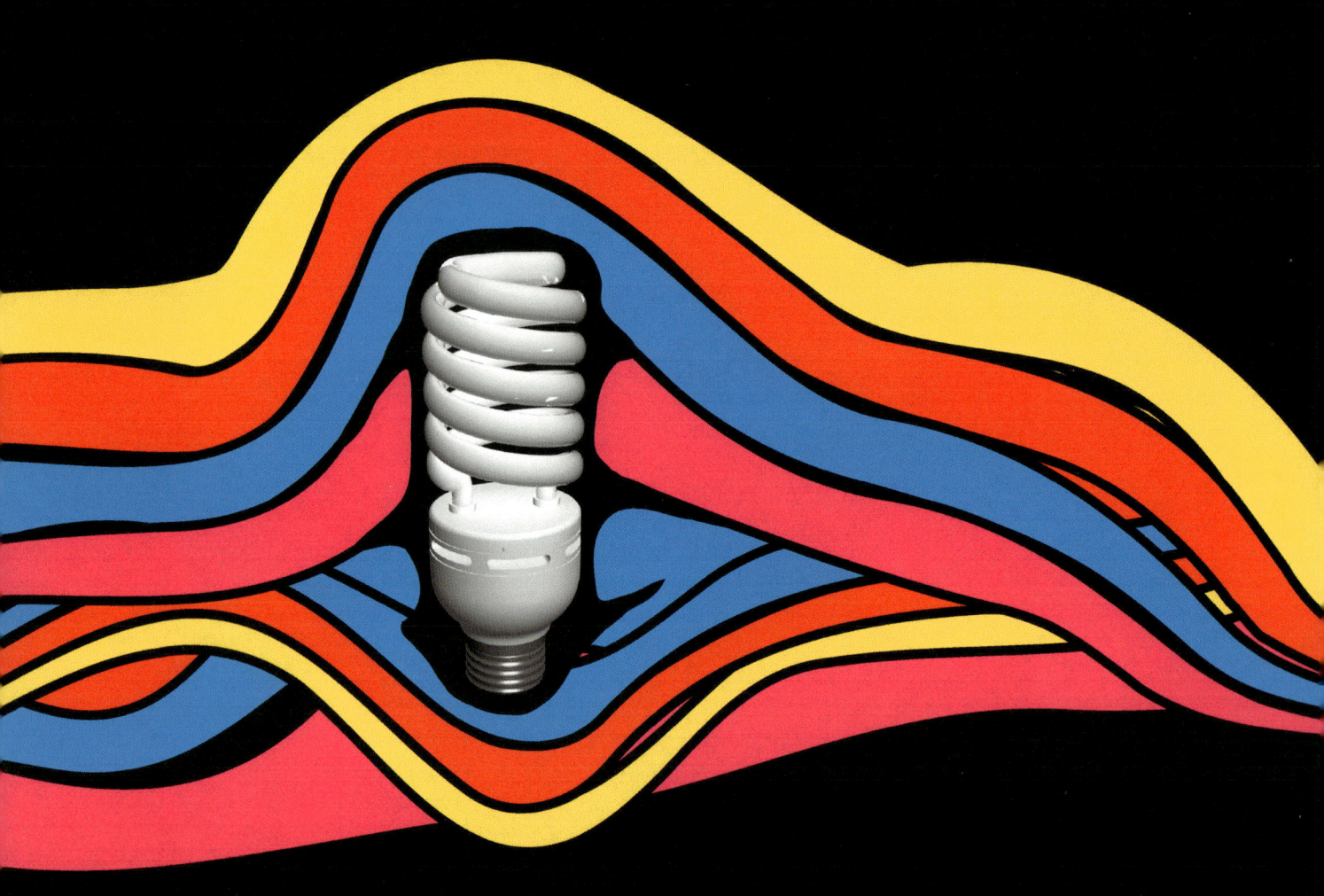

Turn out the light, so you can see the twinkling stars at night.

Feed the big blue recycle eater; he gets very hungry.

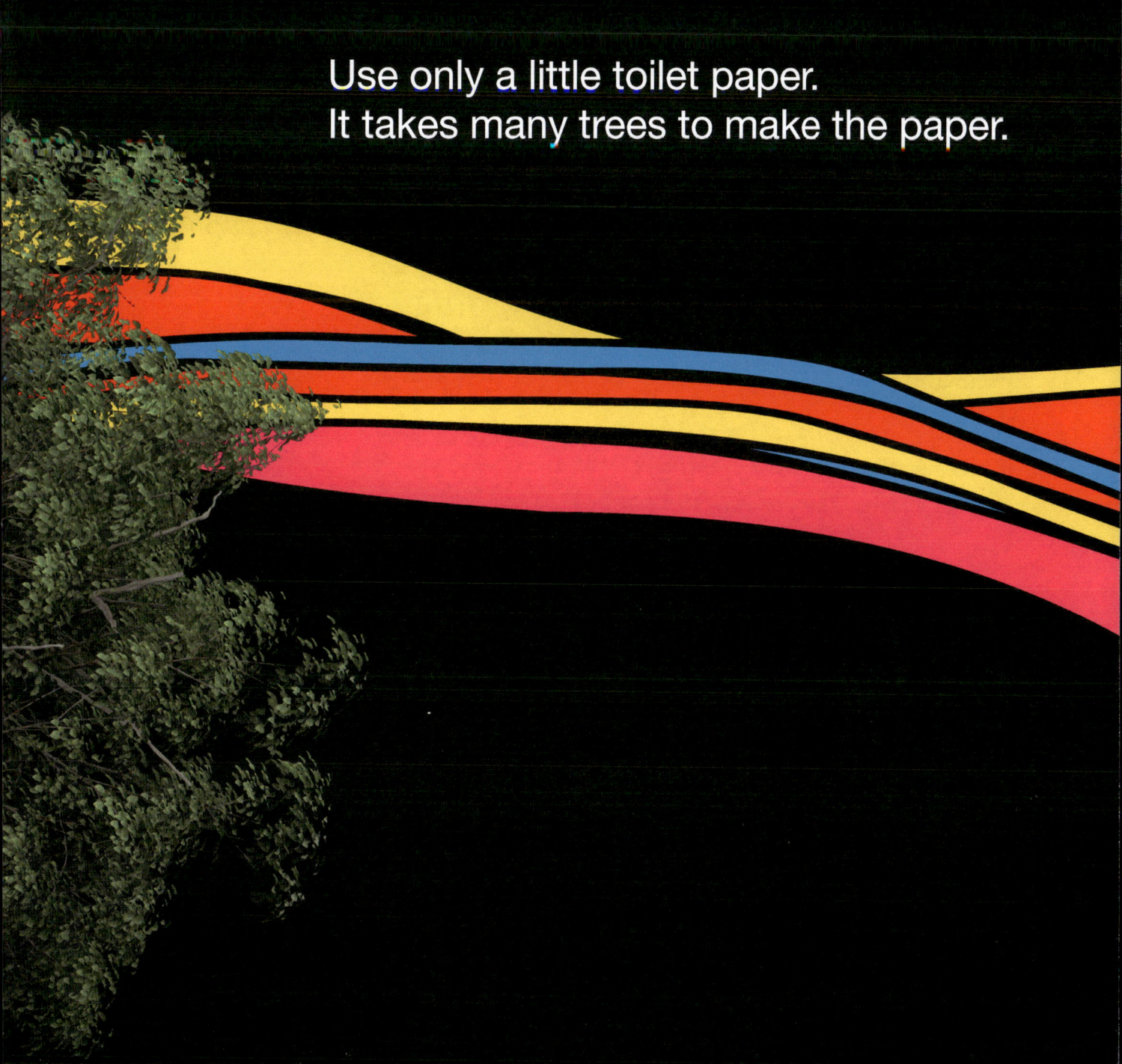

Save energy! Turn the switch off when you're not using your stuff.

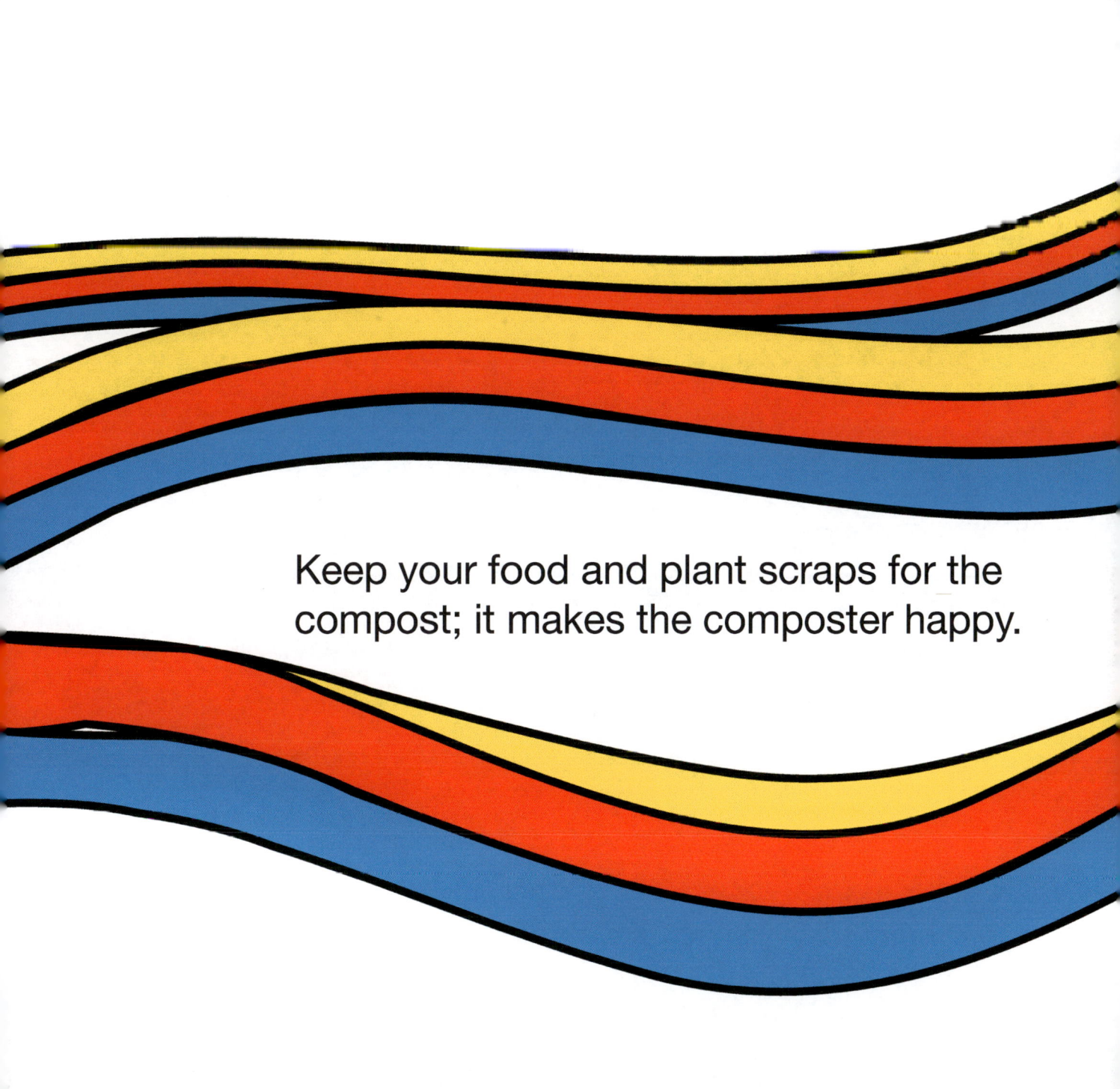
Keep your food and plant scraps for the compost; it makes the composter happy.

Ride your bicycle to the store. It's more fun!

Planting a tree is a good thing.
Trees make air for you to breathe.

10 GOOD IDEAS FOR ADULTS

You can help to switch off global warming and start today - by using clean energy and cutting down on wasted energy.

1. SWITCH TO RENEWABLE ENERGY
Buy non-polluting green electricity from your electricity company. If they don't sell it, can you change power companies to one that does? Get your school, company or community to buy renewable energy, too.

2. BUY ENERGY EFFICIENT APPLIANCES
If you're buying a washing machine, refrigerator, dish washer or oven, buy the most energy-efficient model you can afford. They might be more expensive but they pay for themselves through lower energy bills. The same is true for office equipment like computers, copiers, printers.

3. FLUORESCENT LAMPS ARE CHEAPER IN THE LONG RUN
Replace the lights you use most with compact fluorescent lamps. They cost more than ordinary lamps but you end up saving money because they use only around one-quarter of the electricity to prove the same light. And they last four times as long as a normal light bulb!

4. AVOID STAND-BY AND TURN OFF LIGHTS
Turn off televisions, videos, stereos and computers when they are not in use - they can use between 10 and 60% of the power they use when on "stand by". Turn off lights when you don't need them - it saves energy already after a minute or two. Turn off computer screens when you take a break.

5. WASH ECONOMICALLY
Use the washing machine or dish washer only when you have a full load. Use washing powder suitable for low temperature washes and use economy programmes.

6. ABOUT YOUR FRIDGE
Don't leave fridge doors open for longer than necessary, let food cool down fully before putting it in the fridge or freezer, defrost regularly and keep at the right temperature. Where possible don't stand cookers and fridges/freezers next to each other.

7. GETTING AROUND AND ON YOUR WAY TO WORK AND SCHOOL
When you want to make short journeys, try walking! Use a bicycle for short trips and local shopping. It keeps you fit too and is fun too! Make more use of public transport, such as buses and trains, for longer journeys. Share care journeys with work colleagues or friends - up to a third of car mileage is accounted for by the drive to work.

8. ABOUT YOUR CAR
If you have to buy a car, buy a fuel-efficient, environmentally friendly one. This will save you money and keep more CO_2 from going into the atmosphere. Make sure that your tires are inflated correctly - this can save you 5% on the cost of your petrol. Turn off your engine when waiting in your car.

9. REDUCE YOUR AIR TRAVEL
When you travel to your holiday destination by plane you are contributing to significant emissions of climate change causing carbon dioxide. So take vacations nearer to home, or get there by other forms of transport such as train, bus or boat. If you have to fly, consider buying carbon offsets to compensate for the emissions caused by your flight.

10. ENJOY THE SUN! :-)
Fit solar panels on the roof of your home. Turn your own home into a clean power station!

10 GOOD IDEAS SOURCE - WWF INTERNATIONAL - WWW.PANDA.ORG

A GOOD PLACE TO DRAW YOUR OWN STUFF!

Made in the USA
Charleston, SC
14 May 2012